BRIDGE TECHNIQUE SERIES

DEFENSIVE
SIGNALING

David Bird • Marc Smith

MASTER POINT PRESS • TORONTO

Master Point Press
331 Douglas Ave
Toronto, Ontario, Canada
M5M 1H2
(416) 781-0351   Internet www.masterpointpress.com

Distributed in the USA by Barricade Books
Suite 308a, 185 Bridge Plaza North
Fort Lee, NJ, 07024
(800) 59-BOOKS

Canadian Cataloguing in Publication Data
Bird, David, 1946-
Defensive signaling

(Bridge technique; 8)
ISBN 1-894154-31-2

1. Contract bridge - defensive play. I. Smith, Marc, 1960- . II Title.
III. Series: Bird, David, 1946-. Bridge technique; 8

GV1282.42 B57 2001   795. 41'.53   C00-933112-3

Cover design and Interior: Olena S. Sullivan
Editor: Ray Lee

Printed and bound in Canada

1 2 3 4 5 6 7   07 06 05 04 03 02 01

CONTENTS

Bridge Technique Series

Introduction

Defending is hard, very hard. Many players are good bidders and even more are superb dummy players. Few are exceptional defenders. Anyone who defends even moderately will be a regular winner.

There are three main reasons why defending is so much tougher than declaring. For a start, declarer usually holds the majority of the high cards and, in a suit contract, most of the trumps. He will therefore be on lead most of the time. He can switch tacks as it suits him. Your chances to influence the outcome of the hand as defenders will be far fewer. You will seldom have time to test the water — you or your partner will often have to find the best switch or continuation on your first attempt. It is therefore imperative that you both signal accurately so that the defender who must make the critical decision will be in possession of sufficient information.

Secondly, declarer can see his side's strengths and weaknesses. As a defender, you can see only half of yours. For example, we learn in an early lesson on declarer play to 'lead towards your strength'. As a defender, you will often not even know where that strength lies. Accurate defensive signals can provide this information.

Declarer's final advantage is that he controls both his hand and the dummy. As each of the defenders manages only half of their side's assets, they must work in tandem. It is no good, for example, if one defender is playing to force declarer while the other is trying to set up a defensive ruff — you must work as a partnership. Defensive signals are the tools that enable you to achieve this goal.

You will frequently hear players make comments along the lines of, 'I didn't signal because I didn't want to give information to declarer.' It is true that there are some situations in which a signal will be of more help to declarer than it is to your partner. A good rule to follow is this: *If the information might help your partner to find the best defense later in the hand, you should signal accurately.*

Having established that you want to signal accurately, let's start to look at how you can signal. There are two main methods — attitude signals and count signals. To some extent, they are rival methods and you must choose between them.

The attitude signal

An attitude signal indicates whether you would like partner to continue the suit he has just led. A high spot card says that you like the suit and wish him to continue it. A low spot card denies such interest.

The count signal

A count signal gives no indication as to whether you like the suit that has been led. It merely states whether you have an even or odd number of cards in that suit. A high spot card indicates an even number of cards. A low spot card shows an odd number.

Which method is better?

It has long been generally agreed that it is best to use count signals when declarer plays a suit. He has chosen to play on this suit and it is unlikely that partner wants to know your strength there. Giving count in the played suit, however, will help partner to build up a complete count of the hand, greatly assisting his overall defense.

A decade or so ago, most players favored attitude signals when the defenders led a new suit. Things have changed! Play in a big tournament nowadays and you will find that many contestants use count signals throughout — both in declarer's suits and their own.

In this book we will start by looking closely at both attitude and count signals. We will note the situations where a particular method works well and those where it does not. In Chapter 3 we will see how you can combine the use of attitude signals and count signals, thereby getting the best of both worlds.

Hold on tight and enjoy the ride!

Attitude Signals

It matters little whether one starts to play bridge by attending classes, by reading books or simply by playing with friends, the first defensive signal learned by most players is the basic attitude signal. Using this method, you play a high spot card to tell partner that you like the suit he has led and a low one to tell him that you don't. This method is easy to teach, easy to learn, and easy to understand.

Look at this deal from the West position:

```
Both Vul.              ♠ K Q 4
Dealer South           ♡ 8 6 3
                       ◇ K 5
                       ♣ J 7 6 3 2

♠ 7 6 3                            ♠ 10 8 2
♡ Q J 10 5        N                ♡ K 9 2
◇ Q J 8 2       W   E              ◇ 10 7 6 4 3
♣ K 8             S                ♣ 9 5

                       ♠ A J 9 5
                       ♡ A 7 4
                       ◇ A 9
                       ♣ A Q 10 4
```

WEST	NORTH	EAST	SOUTH
			1♣
pass	3♣	pass	5♣
all pass			

South gives you a chance, by bidding the club game instead of 3NT, and you lead the queen of hearts. Declarer wins with the ace, crosses to dummy with the king of spades, and plays a club to the queen and your king. How do you continue?

The answer is that you cannot tell. It is an unfair question because we have not given you the vital piece of the jigsaw — which heart partner played at Trick 1. Playing attitude signals, partner would have signaled encouragement with the nine of hearts. Placing him with the king of hearts, you would continue that suit to beat the game. A misguided switch to diamonds would allow declarer to throw one of dummy's hearts on his spade suit.

Suppose instead that partner had played a discouraging two of hearts at Trick 1. You would then switch to the queen of diamonds, hoping that he held the ace. Perhaps the full hand would be something like:

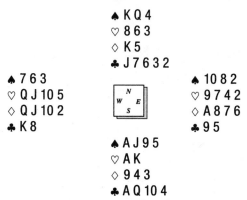

♠ K Q 4
♥ 8 6 3
♦ K 5
♣ J 7 6 3 2

♠ 7 6 3
♥ Q J 10 5
♦ Q J 10 2
♣ K 8

♠ 10 8 2
♥ 9 7 4 2
♦ A 8 7 6
♣ 9 5

♠ A J 9 5
♥ A K
♦ 9 4 3
♣ A Q 10 4

Partner's attitude signal enables you to place the key high cards and beat the contract in both situations.

Defending a suit contract, partner may encourage a continuation because he wants a ruff. Suppose you lead this club suit against South's contract of four hearts.

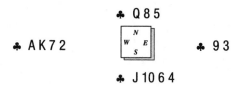

♣ Q 8 5

♣ A K 7 2

♣ 9 3

♣ J 10 6 4

When you lead the ace of clubs, East signals encouragement with the nine. You then cash your second winner and lead a third round of clubs for partner to ruff.

(In this chapter and the next, we assume that you lead the ace from A-K and the king from K-Q. In years gone by, many players led the king from both these holdings. It was not a good method. When partner held J-x-x he had no idea whether to encourage or not.)

Suppose instead that this is the lie of club suit:

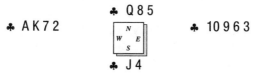

♣ Q 8 5

♣ A K 7 2   ♣ 10 9 6 3

♣ J 4

Partner would play a discouraging three on the first round. You would switch elsewhere, hoping to establish the tricks that were your due before declarer set up a discard on the queen of clubs.

How effective are attitude signals when you lead the top card of a long suit against a notrump contract? Look at this deal:

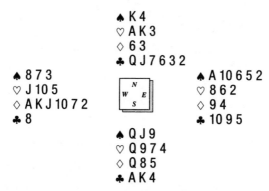

♠ K 4
♡ A K 3
◇ 6 3
♣ Q J 7 6 3 2

♠ 8 7 3   ♠ A 10 6 5 2
♡ J 10 5   ♡ 8 6 2
◇ A K J 10 7 2   ◇ 9 4
♣ 8   ♣ 10 9 5

♠ Q J 9
♡ Q 9 7 4
◇ Q 8 5
♣ A K 4

South opens a weak notrump (12-14 HCP) and is raised to game. You open proceedings with a top diamond. How do you continue if partner, playing attitude signals, follows with the four?

Partner's four of diamonds is the lowest outstanding card in the suit. He would not play a discouraging card if he held the queen, so declarer has that card. If the queen is still guarded (and only count signals could tell you whether or not it is), you must try to put partner on lead to play a second round of diamonds through the queen.

A look at dummy tells you that your partner does not have a fast heart entry. If he holds the ace of clubs, it probably won't matter what you do, so long as you don't play a second diamond. Declarer is unlikely to be able to score nine tricks without touching clubs.

The important case against a guarded queen is when the cards lie as in the diagram. Now you must switch to a spade at Trick 2. Partner will win with his ace and switch back to diamonds. You will take the first seven tricks to beat the contract by three.

Suppose that, on a different layout, partner follows with the nine of diamonds at Trick 1. The nine is the highest missing diamond apart from the queen. Unless the nine is singleton, partner surely has the queen of diamonds. When he holds Q-9-x, you can safely continue with a low diamond to the queen. What if partner started with Q-9 doubleton, though? On lead with the bare queen, he would have no further card in the suit to return.

Some players who use attitude signals in their own suits employ a special method to avoid such blockages, and indeed to detect whether partner does hold an honor in the suit led. They vary which top card they lead from touching honor combinations such as A-K. For example, many Americans play that the lead of an ace against notrump requests partner to unblock any honor they hold, while the lead of a king asks for an attitude signal but not an unblock. Using this method, they would lead the ace from A-K-J-10-x, but the king from A-K-J-x (where an unblock by partner from Q-x or Q-x-x might set up declarer's 10-x-x-x). In Chapter 3 we will recommend a comprehensive system of leads, count signals and attitude signals, which gives you the best possible chance of reading the lie of the suit that has been led.

How do you know when to encourage?

When you are deciding what attitude signal to give, it is not always sufficient to look at your holding in the suit led. Look at this example:

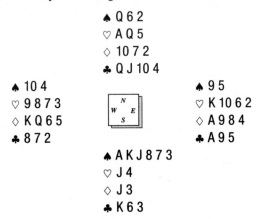

Partner leads the ◇K against four spades. If you look only at the diamond suit, you will play an encouraging nine from the East hand. Partner may well play the ◇5 next, to your ace, and the contract can no longer be beaten! Declarer will win the return, draw trumps, and set up a heart discard on dummy's club suit.

You hold the ace of diamonds, yes, but a grander view of the hand will tell you that a heart switch is needed at Trick 2. You should therefore discourage a diamond continuation by playing the four.

Which spot cards count as a high signal?

You will hear some players say, 'Any card higher than a six is encouraging; a six is neutral and a five or lower is discouraging.' Whether you play attitude or count, any such scheme is a poor one. You can only signal with the spot cards you were dealt! If you hold 10-8-7, the seven is a low card for signaling purposes. If you hold 5-3-2, the five is a high card. Partner must make the effort to determine which spot cards are not on display in his own hand and the dummy. He should assess your signal on that basis.

To see this idea in practice, take the West cards here. You lead the ace of this club suit against a heart contract:

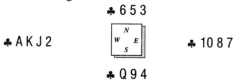

Let's say, first, that the ace draws the three, seven and four. There would not be much sense in saying, 'We play a seven as encouraging', would there? You can see the six, five, three and two; declarer has kindly produced the four. Partner's seven is the lowest spot card out and must therefore be intended as discouraging.

Now suppose that declarer is rather more cunning and follows with the nine on the first round. (He is hiding the four to make your partner's seven look like an encouraging card.) What then? It is now possible, just, that partner is signaling encouragement from Q-7-4. But only if declarer is so wonderfully clever that he has played the nine from 10-9-8! You will encounter few such declarers in your life and it is a much better bet to assume that declarer has the queen. Note that partner cannot hold something like Q-8-7-4. With that holding he would make his signal as clear as possible by playing the eight.

The limitations of attitude signals

Look back briefly to the 3NT contract on page 9. In our discussion of the possible diamond positions we omitted this one:

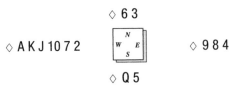

◇ 6 3

◇ A K J 10 7 2　　◇ 9 8 4

◇ Q 5

You lead the ace and partner discourages with the four. Not much help, is it? You know that declarer holds the queen but you have no indication that it is now bare. What you needed in this case was a count signal. If you knew that partner held three diamonds, you could tell that the queen was about to fall.

There is another situation in which attitude signals offer no assistance — when the opening leader holds the top cards in the suit he has led. Suppose you hold the West cards on this deal:

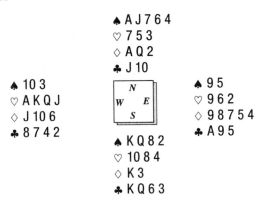

♠ A J 7 6 4
♡ 7 5 3
◇ A Q 2
♣ J 10

♠ 10 3　　　　　　　　　　　♠ 9 5
♡ A K Q J　　　　　　　　　♡ 9 6 2
◇ J 10 6　　　　　　　　　　◇ 9 8 7 5 4
♣ 8 7 4 2　　　　　　　　　♣ A 9 5

♠ K Q 8 2
♡ 10 8 4
◇ K 3
♣ K Q 6 3

You lead the ♡A against South's four spades and partner follows with the two. Not that his discouraging signal comes as much of a surprise — you already knew he had no heart honor. All partner's signal tells you is that he does not hold a doubleton. When you cash a second heart East plays the six. Declarer has followed with the four and the ten. What do you do at Trick 3?

As the cards lie in the diagram above, leading a third heart beats the contract easily. Declarer follows suit and partner's ace of clubs will be the fourth defensive trick.

However, the cards could just as easily lie like this:

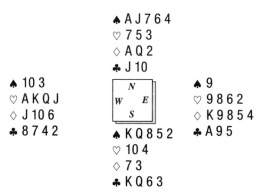

```
              ♠ A J 7 6 4
              ♡ 7 5 3
              ◇ A Q 2
              ♣ J 10
♠ 10 3          ┌─────┐        ♠ 9
♡ A K Q J       │  N  │        ♡ 9 8 6 2
◇ J 10 6      W │     │ E      ◇ K 9 8 5 4
♣ 8 7 4 2       │  S  │        ♣ A 9 5
              └─────┘
              ♠ K Q 8 5 2
              ♡ 10 4
              ◇ 7 3
              ♣ K Q 6 3
```

Now you must switch to a diamond at Trick 3, setting up a fourth trick for the defense. If, instead, you play a third round of hearts, declarer will ruff, draw trumps and set up his clubs. Dummy's diamond losers will disappear on South's club winners.

There are even some hands where a club switch would be needed at Trick 3 (if declarer's minors are ◇K-x-x-x and ♣Q-x, for example). Fear ye not! By the time you have fought your way through to the end of this book, you will be able to beat the contract in all three cases.

Key points

1. When using attitude signals, you play a high spot card to tell partner that you like the suit he has led and want him to continue that suit. Following with your lowest card is discouraging.

2. In suit contracts, an encouraging signal can be made either with a doubleton or with a high honor in the suit led.

3. Attitude signals are popular because they are simple to understand. They have their limitations, however. Whether you should encourage or not is sometimes a matter of judgement. You will not guess to do the right thing every time.

4. There are several situations where an attitude signal will not tell what you need to know but a count signal would (for example, when declarer holds an honor that you might be able to drop). In the next two chapters we will see how you can get the best out of both types of signal.

QUIZ

In each of the examples below, you have agreed to play attitude signals. (Your method is to lead the ace from A-K, the king from K-Q).

A.

♣ A led

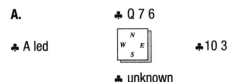

♣ Q 7 6

♣ 10 3

♣ unknown

You are East, defending a major-suit game. Which card do you play when your partner leads the ace of clubs?

B.

♡ K led

♡ A 6 4

♡ J 8 2

♡ unknown

Which heart do you play when partner leads the king and declarer ducks from dummy if you are defending:
i) a club contract?
ii) a notrump contract?

C.

◇ A led

◇ Q 8 6 4

◇ J 7 5 2

◇ unknown

Which diamond do you play when partner leads the ace if you are defending:
i) a spade contract?
ii) a notrump contract?

D.

♠ A 6 4

♠ K led

♠ 8 2

♠ unknown

Defending a contract of four hearts, which spade would you play when partner leads the king and declarer wins with the ace if you hold:

i)   a singleton trump?
ii) three small trumps and dummy has A-K-x-x trumps?
iii) three small trumps and dummy has a singleton trump?

Would any of your answers change if declarer had played low from dummy?

E.

♦ A 9 6

♦ Q led

♦ K J 10 8 5

♦ unknown

Defending a notrump contract, which diamond would you play when partner leads the queen and declarer plays the six from dummy?

F.

♣ 7 6

♣ A led

♣ Q J 8 3

♣ unknown

Defending a spade contract, which club do you play as East when your partner leads the ace?

Answers

A. Play the ten, encouraging. Leading an unsupported ace is rarely a good idea and you can assume that your partner has led from the ace-king. You want him to continue the suit so that you can ruff the third round.

B. i) Play the eight, encouraging. Partner has led from the king-queen and you want him to continue the suit. If you discourage, he will think declarer holds the jack and will switch to avoid giving declarer a second heart trick.

ii) Play the eight for the same reason. Whether you are defending a suit or a notrump contract makes no difference is this case.

C. i) Play the two. Although you hold an honor in the suit led, you want to warn your partner that it is dangerous for him to play the king next. It is quite likely that declarer has only a singleton diamond, in which case he will ruff the king, establishing dummy's queen for a discard in the process. Even if South holds two diamonds, it will not generally be beneficial for the defenders to cash a second round at this stage, setting up the queen.

ii) Play the seven. In notrump you want partner to continue the suit.

D. i) Play the two. Although you have a doubleton, it is highly likely that your trump will have been drawn by the time partner regains the lead. You do not, therefore, want to encourage him to continue spades.

ii) Play the two. For the same reasons as above. Although you hold three trumps this time, dummy's holding suggests that declarer is likely to draw your trumps before partner regains the lead.

iii) Play the eight. Unless declarer has revealed a solid trump suit in the bidding, the odds strongly favor your partner regaining the lead before your trumps are exhausted. Encourage your partner to cash the queen of spades at that point and, if he does not also hold the jack, to give you a third-round ruff.

If instead declarer plays low from dummy, your prime duty is to let partner know whether you hold the jack (to avoid a continuation of the suit running to declarer's jack). You would therefore discourage in all three cases.

E. Play the king. Just because you are playing some kind of signaling method, that's no excuse for not thinking. You can see that overtaking with the king will allow you to drive out dummy's ace, setting up your suit. Perhaps partner's queen is a singleton, in which case he will be unable to continue diamonds. Even if he has a second diamond, he may elect to switch for any one of a number of reasons. If you can see that continuing diamonds is the right thing to do, take control.

F. If you see advantage in gaining the lead, play the queen. This tells your partner that you also hold the jack and he can safely underlead his king of clubs at Trick 2. Otherwise play the eight to encourage partner to cash his second winner.

CHAPTER 2

Count Signals

....

Many players view an attitude signal as a command. Playing at your local club, you will often hear comments such as, 'I told you to lead a heart.' Couched in such terms, the implication is that playing, for example, an encouraging heart tells your partner that leading a heart is the best line of defense. Taking the logic a step further suggests that the signaler can always see the best line of defense and that his partner is expected to follow his instruction blindly.

Let's analyze this thinking further. Each defender can see twenty-six cards, those in his own hand and those in the dummy. There is no particular reason why one defender or the other should be better able to spot the correct line of defense.

Approaching this from a different angle, it seems certain that a single defender will have the best chance of finding the correct defense if, as well as being able to see twenty-six cards, he is also told something about his partner's hand. When you make a signal you should therefore aim to inform partner about your hand, rather than telling him what to do. If you can let him know what you hold, he will be able to work out the best line of defense himself. This concept is crucial.

We discovered in Chapter 2 that attitude signals work only in a limited number of situations. A primary reason for this is that you must make a decision — encourage or discourage. You must express an opinion and you must make that decision alone.

In this chapter we will look at a quite different method of signaling, one in which you show your count (whether you have an even or odd number of cards in the suit). A high spot card will show an even number of cards; a low spot card an odd number.

....

Showing count does not require a subjective decision — you count your cards and tell partner how many you have. It is then up to him to choose a line of defense based on the cards he can see, coupled with what he has learned about your hand.

Inexperienced players often find it hard to believe that it is possible to defend accurately without attitude signals. From the day they first played, they have been fed a regular diet of instructions from their partner — lead this suit, don't continue that suit, etc. Trying to defend without such signals may take some getting used to but the effort is well worthwhile. And it is an effort, because you can no longer look at partner's signal and simply do as you are told. You will actually have to work out the best defense for yourself.

Signaling count when declarer leads a suit

Most players are familiar with the basic principles of count signals. No doubt you already use them when declarer plays a suit, so let's start our discussion there.

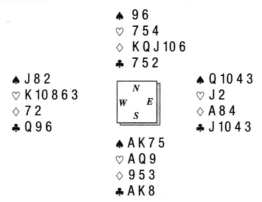

```
              ♠ 9 6
              ♡ 7 5 4
              ◇ K Q J 10 6
              ♣ 7 5 2
♠ J 8 2                        ♠ Q 10 4 3
♡ K 10 8 6 3       N           ♡ J 2
◇ 7 2          W       E       ◇ A 8 4
♣ Q 9 6            S           ♣ J 10 4 3
              ♠ A K 7 5
              ♡ A Q 9
              ◇ 9 5 3
              ♣ A K 8
```

After a 2NT-3NT auction, partner leads the ♡6 to your jack and declarer's queen. Declarer plays a diamond to the king, which you allow to win, and continues with the queen of diamonds. Do you hold up again or take the trick?

You cannot answer the question unless you know how many diamonds declarer holds. If he started with two diamonds, you must win the trick. If he started with three, you must hold up again. To give you the information you need, partner will signal his own length in diamonds. Here he would play the seven on the first round, a high spot card to indicate an even number of diamonds. Even though you have not seen a second card from partner at the time you have to make the key decision, you will know that the seven cannot be a bottom card from three. It is either a singleton (when your own play will make no difference), or from a doubleton. In the latter case declarer will hold three diamonds and you must hold up your ace a second time.

What if this had been the lie of the diamond suit?

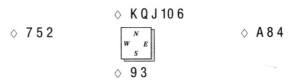

$\diamond$ K Q J 10 6

$\diamond$ 7 5 2

$\diamond$ A 8 4

$\diamond$ 9 3

Partner would have shown an odd number of cards by playing the two. You would therefore take your ace on the second round, rather than the third. Ducking a second time would allow declarer to steal a trick to which he was not entitled.

Signaling count on declarer's suits can have other, less direct, benefits. The defenders can eventually build up a total picture of how the four suits are distributed. This will allow them to discard accurately, keeping the right cards for the endgame.

On the next deal a count signal by one defender tells his partner how many winners declarer has in the suit. Armed with this information, he can then find the correct defense.

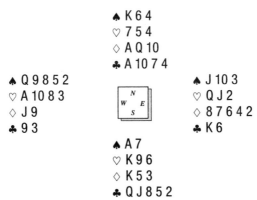

♠ K 6 4
♡ 7 5 4
$\diamond$ A Q 10
♣ A 10 7 4

♠ Q 9 8 5 2
♡ A 10 8 3
$\diamond$ J 9
♣ 9 3

♠ J 10 3
♡ Q J 2
$\diamond$ 8 7 6 4 2
♣ K 6

♠ A 7
♡ K 9 6
$\diamond$ K 5 3
♣ Q J 8 5 2

South opens a weak (12-14) 1NT and is raised to 3NT. You are sitting East and your partner leads the ♠5 to the four, ten and ace. When declarer runs the queen of clubs to your king, partner shows his doubleton in the suit by playing the nine. (We will discuss in a later section how you can distinguish between two cards and four.) What will you do next?

If you pause to count declarer's tricks, you will find that he has at least two spades, three diamonds (finessing if necessary) and four clubs. You know he has four club tricks because of partner's ♣9. That is a total of nine! There is no time to knock out declarer's last spade stopper. You must switch in a hurry to hearts, hoping for four tricks there. Declarer will not like the look of your ♡Q at all!

Do not save declarer a guess

In general, the value of a count signal to your partner will outweigh any benefit that declarer can draw from it. However, this will not be the case when you save declarer a guess in the suit itself. Suppose South has to tackle this club suit:

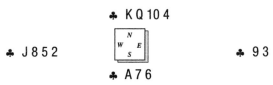

♣ K Q 10 4

♣ J 8 5 2   ♣ 9 3

♣ A 7 6

He begins with a low card to dummy's king. West can see that there is likely to be an impending guess in the suit. Even if the defending side uses count signals in general, it will be obvious to West to disguise his holding by playing the two. What if East gives the matter insufficient attention and signals count with the nine? This will also give the game away. When declarer continues with the four to his ace, East's three will show. Declarer is then likely to finesse dummy's ten, scoring four tricks in the suit.

'But I might have been fooling him by playing the nine from J-9-3,' East will say.

As most declarers know, for every opponent who tries the nine from J-9-3, there are at least ten less able defenders who will play the nine from 9-3!

Signaling count when our side leads a suit

Many tournament players nowadays use count signals on their own suits, as well as on declarer's. There are times when this information is more useful than that given by an attitude signal. Indeed, knowing partner's length in a suit will frequently make the defense very easy.

Take the West seat on our next deal. Cover the East and South cards if you want to challenge yourself:

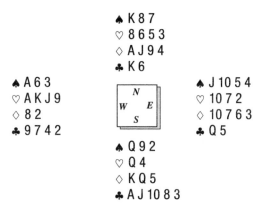

```
              ♠ K 8 7
              ♡ 8 6 5 3
              ◇ A J 9 4
              ♣ K 6
♠ A 6 3                          ♠ J 10 5 4
♡ A K J 9        N               ♡ 10 7 2
◇ 8 2        W       E           ◇ 10 7 6 3
♣ 9 7 4 2        S               ♣ Q 5
              ♠ Q 9 2
              ♡ Q 4
              ◇ K Q 5
              ♣ A J 10 8 3
```

South opens a weak (12-14) 1NT and is raised to game. You lead a top heart on which your partner plays the two and declarer the four.

How would you continue if you are playing attitude signals?

What if you were playing count signals?

Playing attitude signals, you can place declarer with the queen of hearts. You have little idea what to do next, though. If the queen is doubleton, you need to continue with the king of hearts. If declarer started with queen third in hearts, you must reach partner's hand in some other suit, so he can lead a second round of hearts through the queen. In other words, the correct defense is a complete guess!

Playing count signals, the defense is straightforward. Ask yourself: 'from what heart holdings would partner play the two?'

The three-card possibilities are Q-10-2, Q-7-2, 10-7-2, 10-4-2 and 7-4-2. Whichever of these holdings partner has, continuing with a second high heart will defeat the contract. If partner began with queen third, South's spot card will appear under your king. You will continue with a third heart to partner's queen, regain the lead with the ace of spades, and cash your fourth heart winner as the setting trick. If instead the queen of hearts is doubleton in declarer's hand, it will fall under your king. Your jack and nine of hearts, followed by the spade ace, will put the contract one down.

The only other possibility is that East holds Q-2 doubleton. In Chapter 3 we will cover the subject of whether the defender in third seat should unblock any honor that he holds. Here, as you can see, you can survive the lack of an unblock. When you cashed your remaining top honor, partner's queen would fall. Your jack and nine would then score.

Are you ready to try another one? Again, you are West. Cover the East and South cards:

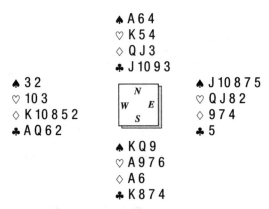

```
              ♠ A 6 4
              ♡ K 5 4
              ◇ Q J 3
              ♣ J 10 9 3
♠ 3 2                        ♠ J 10 8 7 5
♡ 10 3          N           ♡ Q J 8 2
◇ K 10 8 5 2  W   E         ◇ 9 7 4
♣ A Q 6 2       S           ♣ 5
              ♠ K Q 9
              ♡ A 9 7 6
              ◇ A 6
              ♣ K 8 7 4
```

South opens with a strong (15-17) notrump and North raises to game. You lead the ◇5, won in dummy with the queen. Partner follows with the four and South with the six. Declarer then runs the jack of clubs to your queen. How would you defend?

Playing attitude signals, you know only that your partner does not hold the ace of diamonds. Not very useful, is it? You knew that already when dummy's queen won! Once again, you will have to guess the best defense. If declarer's ace of diamonds is now bare, you can dislodge it while you still hold the club ace. If declarer started with ace third in diamonds, though, you may need to find partner with the ace of hearts. A heart switch would then allow him to play diamonds from his side of the table, setting up the suit.

You are much better placed if you are playing count signals. Here partner will play the ◇4 on the first trick. If this is a singleton, it is most unlikely that you can beat the contract. Your best chance is to continue the suit, hoping that partner has three diamonds. If instead partner had played the ◇9 or ◇7 on the first trick, suggesting a doubleton, you would place declarer with ace third in the suit. A heart switch would be indicated.

Good bridge players hate having to guess! That's one reason why so many of them like to play count signals.

Does partner hold four cards or two?

When you are signaling count from a doubleton, you have no choice regarding which cards you play. You start with the higher one, then play the lower one. Which cards should you choose when you hold four cards? It may not seem to matter but, by following a standard agreement, you can give partner an excellent chance of detecting whether you hold four cards or two.

To show count from four cards, generally play
the second-best card followed by the third-best

Suppose you hold ◇9742. When this suit is led (and you do not have to play high to try to win the trick) you should follow with the seven. It is always a good principle to signal 'loudly'. If you start your high-low with the four, partner will not be able to tell whether you are starting an echo or playing low from three cards. Remember, he may have to take the crucial decision before he sees your second card. Make the message as clear as possible with the first.

'Why not the top card first?' you may be wondering. Often you cannot afford your highest card. Even here, the nine may have a role to play. Indeed, it is an important principle of signaling that you should never signal with a card that you cannot afford.

On the second round you will play the four, your third-best card. Knowing that you will choose your cards in this way from a four-card holding nearly always allows your partner to detect whether you hold four or two cards. Let's see how this works in practice.

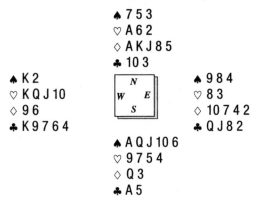

```
                    ♠ 7 5 3
                    ♡ A 6 2
                    ◇ A K J 8 5
                    ♣ 10 3
  ♠ K 2                              ♠ 9 8 4
  ♡ K Q J 10        N                ♡ 8 3
  ◇ 9 6          W      E            ◇ 10 7 4 2
  ♣ K 9 7 6 4       S                ♣ Q J 8 2
                    ♠ A Q J 10 6
                    ♡ 9 7 5 4
                    ◇ Q 3
                    ♣ A 5
```

After an enemy auction of 1◇-1♠, 2♠-4♠, you lead the ♡K. Let's assume that you are playing count signals. Declarer ducks the first round in dummy and partner plays the eight. When you continue with a second heart, declarer puts up the ace and your partner produces the three. A trump is played to the queen and your king and you must now decide what to do.

Partner's echo tells you that he started with either four hearts or two. If he had only two hearts, you will want to cash a third heart and lead a fourth round to give partner an overruff. If instead partner has four hearts, you will want to switch to clubs (hoping that partner holds the club ace, or both minor-suit queens.) How can you tell?

Look at the cards that partner has played; he played the eight and the three. Since the three is the lowest spot-card out, these cannot possibly be the second- and third-best cards from four. So, you continue with hearts and beat the contract.

You will rarely be in any doubt as to whether partner holds four cards or two. Suppose the heart suit had lain like this:

♡ A 6 2

♡ K Q J 10 | N / W   E / S | ♡ 7 4

♡ 9 8 5 3

Declarer would have to play the five, followed by the eight or nine, to introduce any doubt. Are your opponents that clever? Even when there is an ambiguity, the bidding will often give you a clue.

Look back for a last time at the full diagram for that 4♠ contract. If you were playing attitude signals you would have to discourage from four small, three small or two small, in case partner was leading from K-Q-10-x and was in danger of continuing the suit to South's jack. You can see how little help this would give partner, with his actual holding.

It has probably occurred to you by now that playing count signals can be hard work. No longer can you look at your partner's card and just continue or not as he instructs. You actually have to work out the best defense for yourself. The upside is that you will be able to do so fairly often. The major aspect of count signaling that may take a little getting used to is watching the spot cards carefully. Playing attitude signals, these cards are just 'high' or 'low'. Playing count, as you can see from the examples above, the precise spot will often be the key.

Signaling from an honor sequence

When you wish to indicate a sequence of honors, either with a signal or (as we will see later) with a discard, it is traditional to play the highest card in the sequence.

◇ A 8 6

◇ 7 led | N / W   E / S | ◇ K Q J 3

◇ unknown

If declarer rises with dummy's ace, you could play the king to indicate possession of the queen and jack. If instead you were to play the queen, this would deny the king and suggest a holding headed by the Q-J-10. A signal with an honor has this same meaning whether your general method is attitude or count.

Defending a trump contract, suppose partner leads from a suit headed by the A-K combination and you have Q-J-x or Q-J-x-x in the suit. If you want to gain the lead on the next trick, you should signal with the queen (rather than giving count with a spot card). This is a common maneuver, gaining heavily on deals such as the following. Take the East cards:

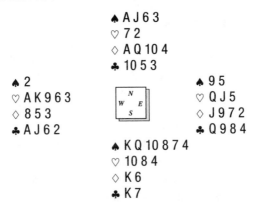

Your partner opens 1♡ but the opponents shrug this aside and bid to 4♠. When the ♡A is led, you can see that it may be beneficial to lead clubs from your side of the table. You signal with the ♡Q, indicating possession of the jack. West duly leads a low heart on the next trick. You win with the jack and a club switch beats the contract.

Remember always that you should be wary of signaling with a card that may cost a trick. Consider this suit:

$$\diamond\ 9\ 6\ 5\ 3$$

$$\diamond\ K\ 7 \qquad \boxed{\begin{array}{c} N \\ W \quad E \\ S \end{array}} \qquad \diamond\ Q\ J\ 10\ 2$$

$$\diamond\ A\ 8\ 4$$

South arrives in a major-suit game and partner tries his luck with a doubleton king of diamonds. If you signal your sequence by playing the queen you may find that declarer draws trumps and eventually generates his tenth trick from the diamond suit. You may still decide to play the queen, hoping that partner has a trump trick and will then be in no doubt what to do next. There is a possible cost attached, however.

Signaling count when returning partner's suit

To conclude our look at basic count signals we must also consider how to give count when you are first to play to a trick. You are already familiar with such concepts as 'fourth-best leads' and the 'Rule of Eleven'. What about when you are returning partner's suit, though?

When returning partner's suit, play your higher card when you have two cards remaining, otherwise your original fourth-best.

Let's see a full-deal example of this straight away:

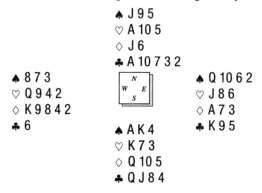

♠ J 9 5
♡ A 10 5
◇ J 6
♣ A 10 7 3 2

♠ 8 7 3
♡ Q 9 4 2
◇ K 9 8 4 2
♣ 6

♠ Q 10 6 2
♡ J 8 6
◇ A 7 3
♣ K 9 5

♠ A K 4
♡ K 7 3
◇ Q 10 5
♣ Q J 8 4

South opens a strong (15-17) notrump and is raised to game. Sitting West, you lead the four of diamonds, East winning with the ace. With two cards in the suit remaining, partner returns the ◇7.

Since the eventual club finesse will be into East's hand, it is essential that you do not surrender your king on the second round of diamonds. You must allow South's card to win, retaining your ◇K as a later entry. Declarer is aware of this and may attempt to fool you by playing the queen on the second round. How should you read the situation then? If declarer's queen is his last card in the suit, partner would have started with ◇A1073. From this holding he would have returned his original fourth-best card, the ◇3. You can therefore be certain that South has another diamond, which can only be the ten. You hold up the king and declarer tumbles to defeat.

It's an important area, worth one more example. Try your luck with the West cards here:

Neither Vul.   ♠ A Q 8 2
Dealer South   ♡ 8 4
        ◇ Q 7 5 2
        ♣ K 8 3

```
♠ J 7 6 3              ♠ 9 5
♡ A 10 7 5 2      N    ♡ K J 6 3
◇ 9 3          W     E ◇ J 6 4
♣ J 9              S   ♣ Q 10 5 4
```

        ♠ K 10 4
        ♡ Q 9
        ◇ A K 10 8
        ♣ A 7 6 2

WEST	NORTH	EAST	SOUTH
			1NT (15-17)
pass	2♣	pass	2◇
pass	3NT	all pass	

You lead the ♡5 against 3NT and partner wins with the king. His return of the ♡3 is covered by South's queen. Assuming you were at the table and could not see that the queen was South's last card in the suit (!), how would you judge the situation?

A hold-up would be beneficial only if South had begun with Q-J-9 in the heart suit. This would leave your partner with K-6-3, and from that holding he would have returned the six. Partner's ♡3 can only be from K-J-6-3 or K-3 doubleton. On this particular hand you can rule out the second possibility because of South's Stayman response. You therefore know that South started with a doubleton heart.

Even if the bidding had been less revealing, say 1NT-3NT, you would have nothing to lose by winning with the ace and returning the seven. In situations where you actually do need to tell the difference between four and two cards with declarer, look at the spot card he played on the first round. On this hand, for example, he played the nine. Would he have chosen this card when holding Q-9-6-3? He would not. Such a play might give away a second stopper in the suit. In the long term you will gain heavily by assuming that declarer is playing his spot cards from the bottom.

Before we leave this point we must issue one word of warning. Blindly returning your fourth-best card may not always be sufficient to resolve partner's problems. The following, comical situation actually happened in a world championship:

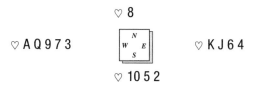

♡ 8

♡ A Q 9 7 3   ♡ K J 6 4

♡ 10 5 2

West, having led the ♡7 against 3NT, was pleased to see his partner win with the king. Declarer, meanwhile, contributed the five. Giving the matter little thought, East returned a textbook ♡4, his original fourth best. South played the ten and West won with the queen. The seconds ticked by as West considered his next play. Eventually he switched to a different suit and the contract was made. Who was to blame for this accident, would you say?

It was not West's fault. After declarer's cunning retention of the ♡2, West placed his partner with an original K-4-2. If that were the case, the heart suit would look like this:

♡ 8

♡ A Q 9 7 3   ♡ K 4 2

♡ J 10 6 5

It would now be correct for West to switch elsewhere, hoping to find his partner's outside entry so that he could lead the third round of hearts through declarer's remaining J-6.

East's return of the four was wooden — it could never cost to return the jack. Declarer was marked, by the Rule of Eleven, with one card higher than the seven. If this were the ace, West's remaining cards would be ready to cash when he gained the lead. If it were not the ace, the suit would run immediately.

There are two other situations where it may be dangerous to return your fourth-best card. The first occurs when doing so may block the suit. That's the case here:

♠ 3

♠ A 7 6 4 2   ♠ K 10 8 5

♠ Q J 9

West leads the ♠4 against 3NT and you win with the king. If you return the five, South playing the queen, there is no way that you can enjoy four spade winners. Whether or not West holds up his ace on the second round, one of your remaining spot cards will win the fourth round of the suit. Partner's last spade will wither on the vine. You should return the ten, despite the fact that this may cause partner to mis-read the count.

The other situation is when you may need to retain the lead to play a third round of the suit.

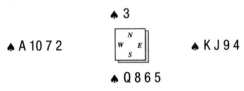

♠ 3

♠ A 10 7 2   ♠ K J 9 4

♠ Q 8 6 5

Partner leads the ♠2, won by your king. Since partner can hold only four spades, you are not concerned with a potential blockage in the suit. Suppose you return the ♠4, however. Declarer will cover with one of his spot cards and your partner will now be on lead. Unless there is an outside entry to your hand, declarer's queen will be promoted into a stopper. Return the ♠J on the second round and there will be no such problem.

The limitations of count signals

If count signals were perfect in all situations, no-one in the world would still be using attitude signals. To present a balanced picture, it is right that we should look at some situations where attitude signals work better than count signals. This does not mean that you will have to toler-ate such limitations. Indeed, in the very next chapter we will see how you can combine the benefits of both types of signal.

You would like to be playing attitude in this situation:

♠ A 8 3

♠ K Q 10 2   ♠ 9 6 4

♠ J 7 5

You lead the ♠K, either against a suit contract or one in notrump. If you are playing count signals, partner will contribute the four. Not much use, is it? If he holds the jack you will want to continue the suit. If declarer has the jack, a continuation will surrender a trick. An attitude signal would let you know if partner held the jack. It's true, when defending notrump at any rate, that partner could probably afford to unblock the jack if he held it. Against a suit contract, such an unblock might cost a trick if partner had led from K-Q-x.

An attitude signal might be more useful than count here, too:

♠ A 8 3

♠ Q 10 7 5 4   [W N E S]   ♠ K 9 2

♠ J 6

You lead the ♠5 against a heart contract and declarer rises with the ace. On some deals you would like to know whether partner holds the king.

Against that, count is more useful here:

♠ A 10 3

♠ K J 7 5 4   [W N E S]   ♠ Q 9 2

♠ 8 6

You lead the ♠5 against a suit contract and the trick is won with dummy's ace. If partner gives you a count signal of the two, you know the whole position in the suit. Declarer would surely have let the lead run to his queen, if he held it. Your partner must therefore hold queen third. An attitude signal (here the nine) would tell you about the queen. It would not tell you whether you had a cashable trick in the suit.

Key points

1. Count signals can work well whether it is declarer or partner who has led the suit. You can signal your length whenever you are not trying to win a trick.

2. Playing high-low shows an even number of cards in the suit played. Following upwards indicates an odd number.

3. When signaling length from four cards, start with your second highest, then play your original third-best on the second round.

4. Preserving potential winners always takes precedence over signaling. Do not signal with a card you may not be able to afford.

5. When partner signals his length at Trick 1, work out his possible holdings in the suit. You will often find that a particular line of defense will work no matter which of those possible holdings he has.

6. When returning partner's suit, play the higher card from two remaining, otherwise your original fourth-best.

7. It is easy to signal woodenly, without thinking, when playing count. After all, what could be easier than counting your cards and signaling either an odd or even number? Be aware of the small number of situations in which your signal may be ambiguous to partner or may cause problems of communication.

In each of the examples below, assume you have agreed to play count signals. (As before, you also lead the ace from ace-king.)

A.   ♣ Q 7 6 4

♣ A led      ♣ 10 9 8 3

♣ unknown

Defending a spade contract, which club do you play as East when your partner leads the ace?

B.   ♡ 8 6 4

♡ A led      ♡ Q 7 2

♡ unknown

Defending a spade contract, which heart do you play when your partner leads the ace?

C.   ♢ 8 6 4

♢ A led      ♢ Q 2

♢ unknown

Defending a heart contract, which diamond do you play when your partner leads the ace?

D.   ♠ A 6 4

♠ K led      ♠ 9 7 5 2

♠ unknown

Defending a diamond contract, which spade do you play when your partner leads the king?

E.   ◇ Q J 5 3

◇ A K 7 4   N W E S   ◇ 8 played

◇ 2 played

You lead the ace of diamonds against a spade contract.

    i) How do the diamonds lie?

    ii) What is likely to be the best continuation?

F.   ♣ 10 8 6 4

♣ A K J 5   N W E S   ♣ 3 played

♣ 7 played

You lead the ace of clubs against a spade contract.

    i) How do the clubs lie?

    ii) What is likely to be the best continuation?

G.   ♡ A 7 4

♡ K Q 10 5 3   N W E S   ♡ 6 played

♡ 2 played

You lead the king of hearts against a notrump contract.

    i) How do the hearts lie?

    ii) What is likely to be the best continuation?

H.   ◇ 10 4

◇ 5 led   N W E S   ◇ A J 6 3

◇ 2 played

Partner leads the five of diamonds against a notrump contract. After winning with the ace, which diamond do you return?

Answers

A. Play the nine. The most likely scenario is that declarer holds a singleton club. In that case, you must try to warn your partner about continuing with the king. It is therefore imperative that you play an accurate count card — second highest from four.

B. Play the two. Do not think that playing the seven will tell your partner that you hold the queen. It won't — all it will tell him is that you hold an even number of hearts. That misinformation may guide him away from the winning defense. Give a true count and trust your partner to work out how best to proceed.

C. Play the two. You will recall that playing the queen under partner's king tells him that he can underlead his ace to your jack on the second round if he so wishes. Clearly, you do not want him to try that this time, so follow with the two. Partner is well aware that this is a possible holding when you follow with the two.

D. Play the seven. Even though you hold no honor in the suit do not worry that partner will think you are encouraging him. From four cards you follow with your second highest. Partner knows that and will work out the best defense as long as you provide him with accurate information about your hand.

E. i) Partner has fewer than four diamonds. If declarer's two were singleton, this would leave your partner with ◊ 10-9-8-6. From that holding he would play the nine, not the eight. Partner's diamonds are either ◊ 10-9-8, ◊ 8-6 doubleton, or singleton ◊ 8.

ii) Unless you can see an alternative source of tricks, your best chance is probably to continue with the king of diamonds and hope to give partner a third-round ruff.

F. i) Partner's possible club holdings are Q-9-3, Q-3, 3-2 and singleton 3.

ii) In all cases, the best defense is likely to be cashing the king of clubs next. If partner started with a doubleton or singleton, you can give him a ruff next. If he began with ♣Q-9-3, you will have to decide at Trick 3 whether you want to force declarer or shift your attentions elsewhere.

G. i) You can probably tell from the bidding that partner's ♡6 is not a singleton. He must, therefore, hold three hearts. You do not know if these include the jack but that is irrelevant.

ii) Continue with the queen of hearts. This will kill declarer's doubleton jack if that is his holding. If partner has the jack, two things might happen. Declarer will probably duck the ace again and, if so, you can simply clear the suit. If declarer does rise with the ace, then partner should realize that you hold the ten and that he should unblock.

H. If you were going to give count, you would return the three of diamonds. You cannot afford that luxury here though. The suit could easily lie like this:

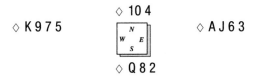

◇ 10 4

◇ K 9 7 5   ◇ A J 6 3

◇ Q 8 2

Returning the three allows declarer to score a trick in the suit (by guessing to play low on the second round). You must return the jack to kill the power of dummy's ten.

CHAPTER 3

Combining Count and Attitude Signals

In the last two chapters we have seen both pluses and minuses of the two primary signaling methods. Now let's see if we can use them in a way that combines the best of both schemes.

What sort of signal would be most useful when you lead from an ace-king combination against a major-suit game? If you were leading from ♣AK5, you would like an attitude signal. If you were leading from ♣AK10762, a count signal could be more useful — it would tell you whether a second round would stand up.

Similarly, what sort of signal would you like when you are leading from ◇KQ102 against a major-suit game? An attitude signal would save you from falling for a Bath Coup (a continuation of the suit when declarer ducked from A-J-x). If instead you were leading from a holding such as ◇KQJ53, a count signal would be more useful. Even if declarer won the trick, you would know how many winners you could cash when you regained the lead.

We are going to recommend a system of honor card leads that will allow you to ask partner for either an attitude signal or a count signal, whichever you think you need. It is probably not the system you were taught to play, but it has two immense advantages: 1) it works extremely well, and 2) it is easy to remember, because you can use the same method against both suits and notrump. This is the scheme:

> *Lead the ace or queen to ask for an attitude signal.*
> *Lead the king to ask for a count signal.*

This applies against both notrump contracts and suit contracts.

So, when you are leading from a combination headed by the A-K or K-Q you choose which honor to lead, according to which signal you would like. Clever, eh? Let's see some examples of this method in operation.

Asking for count when leading a long suit

Minor honors in side suits are frequently irrelevant because someone will be able to ruff the third round of the suit. For this reason, you will usually need a count signal when you lead from a long suit. Look at the next deal from the West position:

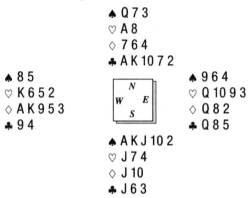

                    ♠ Q 7 3
                    ♡ A 8
                    ◇ 7 6 4
                    ♣ A K 10 7 2
    ♠ 8 5   ♠ 9 6 4
    ♡ K 6 5 2   N   ♡ Q 10 9 3
    ◇ A K 9 5 3   W   E   ◇ Q 8 2
    ♣ 9 4   S   ♣ Q 8 5
                    ♠ A K J 10 2
                    ♡ J 7 4
                    ◇ J 10
                    ♣ J 6 3

You lead a top diamond against four spades. Suppose you choose to lead the ace, to request an attitude signal. East will follow with the eight, declarer with the ten. You continue with the king, on which partner completes his echo with the two and declarer plays the jack. How should you continue?

The answer is that you have no idea. Your partner would play an encouraging high-low from both ◇Q82 and ◇82 doubleton. On the actual layout, you must switch to a heart at Trick 3. Playing a third diamond would allow declarer to score ten tricks. If instead East held a doubleton diamond and no ♡Q, you would need to give him a ruff.

When you lead from a five-card or longer suit, it is more likely that a count signal will be helpful. Here you should lead the king of diamonds, requesting a count signal. If the cards lie as in the diagram, partner will signal with the two. You will cash one more diamond, then switch to hearts. When partner holds ◇82 instead, he will signal with the eight. You will then give him a diamond ruff. A count signal allows you to beat the contract in both cases, with no guesswork involved.

From long suits headed by the ace-king or the king-queen, you should therefore lead the king to ask for a count signal.

Asking for attitude when leading a short suit

The situation is different when you choose to lead from a short suit such as A-K-x or K-Q-x, particularly against a notrump contract. The information you then need is whether partner likes the suit. Take the West seat for this example:

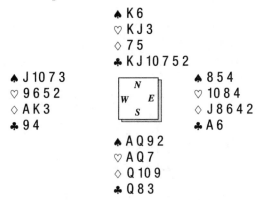

```
                  ♠ K 6
                  ♡ K J 3
                  ◇ 7 5
                  ♣ K J 10 7 5 2
  ♠ J 10 7 3                        ♠ 8 5 4
  ♡ 9 6 5 2          N             ♡ 10 8 4
  ◇ A K 3        W       E         ◇ J 8 6 4 2
  ♣ 9 4             S             ♣ A 6
                  ♠ A Q 9 2
                  ♡ A Q 7
                  ◇ Q 10 9
                  ♣ Q 8 3
```

South opens with a strong notrump (15-17) and North raises to 3NT. Not unreasonably, you elect to survey the scene by leading a high diamond. Since you will need to know whether your partner likes diamonds, you lead the ace to request an attitude signal. East will encourage with the ◇8 and the defense will be plain sailing.

Suppose instead that you request a count signal, by leading the king. Partner would follow with the two of diamonds to show an odd number. What useful information that is — *not*! If you chose to guess that partner held five diamonds and continued with ace and another diamond, the whole hand might look something like this:

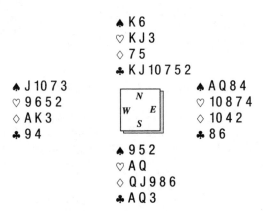

```
              ♠ K 6
              ♡ K J 3
              ◇ 7 5
              ♣ K J 10 7 5 2
♠ J 10 7 3              ♠ A Q 8 4
♡ 9 6 5 2      N        ♡ 10 8 7 4
◇ A K 3    W     E      ◇ 10 4 2
♣ 9 4         S         ♣ 8 6
              ♠ 9 5 2
              ♡ A Q
              ◇ Q J 9 8 6
              ♣ A Q 3
```

Declarer would laugh all the way to the bank as he scored up eleven tricks. A spade switch would have netted the first six tricks for the defense.

Here is one more example of seeking an attitude signal:

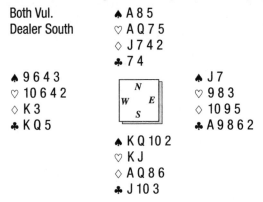

Both Vul.   ♠ A 8 5
Dealer South   ♡ A Q 7 5
              ◇ J 7 4 2
              ♣ 7 4

```
♠ 9 6 4 3              ♠ J 7
♡ 10 6 4 2     N       ♡ 9 8 3
◇ K 3      W     E     ◇ 10 9 5
♣ K Q 5       S        ♣ A 9 8 6 2
              ♠ K Q 10 2
              ♡ K J
              ◇ A Q 8 6
              ♣ J 10 3
```

WEST	NORTH	EAST	SOUTH
			1NT
pass	2♣	pass	2♠
pass	3NT	all pass	

With each of the opponents known to hold a major, you decide to attack with a high club. Suppose you choose the king — partner follows with the two, showing an odd number, and declarer with the three. Does the information help at all? Not a bit. Partner might hold ♣1062, while a cunning declarer lies in wait with ♣AJ983. What you need is an attitude signal. You should therefore lead the queen of clubs.

A queen lead can be from a holding headed by either the K-Q or the

Q-J. Strangely, this does not cause any problems to a partner who has to decide whether to encourage or not. If he holds the king or jack himself, he will know what you hold and will play an encouraging card. If he holds the ace he will encourage anyway, not minding which holding you are leading from. Holding no honor, he will discourage.

The possible ambiguity of a queen lead is also removed, of course, when dummy goes down with the king or jack.

Leading from A-K-x-x

We have already seen that you should usually request count with ace-king fifth, attitude with ace-king third. How about ace-king fourth? You can make your own choice, depending on the contract and the bidding. The lower the opponents' contract and the less distributional their hands appear to be, the more likely it is that an attitude signal will assist. The higher the contract is, the more likely it is that you will want to know if two winners are cashing in the suit. In our experience a count signal is generally more useful. When in doubt, ask for that.

Signaling attitude on an ace

It is generally a poor idea to lead unsupported aces against any contract at the four-level or lower. Indeed, you will not go far wrong if you never make such a lead (unless partner has bid the suit, of course!). It follows that when partner does lead an ace against such a contract, you should base your attitude signal on the assumption that he holds both the ace and the king.

The situation is different when the contract is at the five-level or higher. Since partner will then always lead the king from ace-king, to ask for count and discover whether both his honors will cash, the lead of an ace denies the king! You should therefore signal encouragement only when you hold the king yourself.

Understanding these ideas is vital when you are trying to cash out against a high-level contract. Suppose you are West on this deal:

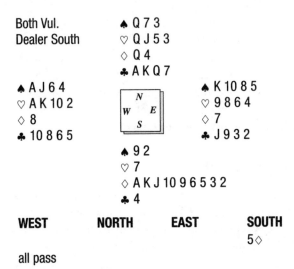

Both Vul.
Dealer South

♠ Q 7 3
♡ Q J 5 3
◇ Q 4
♣ A K Q 7

♠ A J 6 4
♡ A K 10 2
◇ 8
♣ 10 8 6 5

♠ K 10 8 5
♡ 9 8 6 4
◇ 7
♣ J 9 3 2

♠ 9 2
♡ 7
◇ A K J 10 9 6 5 3 2
♣ 4

WEST	NORTH	EAST	SOUTH
			5◇
all pass			

You lead the king of hearts, requesting count. Partner plays the eight (his second-best card) and declarer follows with the seven. Since partner's eight is consistent with a possible four-card holding, you are wary of playing the ace of hearts at this stage. Instead you cash the ace of spades. An ace requests an attitude signal and partner plays the ten. You duly play a second spade, hoping that it will not be ruffed, and defeat the contract. If partner had discouraged on the spade ace, you would have switched back to the king of hearts, hoping that declarer held three cards in the suit rather than one.

Suppose declarer had held one spade and two hearts instead. Your partner would then have shown an odd count on the ♡K lead, telling you that a second heart would stand up. You would have beaten the contract in that case too. Anyone playing attitude signals would have had to guess what to do.

Unblocking after a king lead at notrump

What card would you lead from A-K-x-x-x or A-K-x-x-x-x against a notrump contract? You would normally lead your fourth best. This would avoid any problems of a blockage if partner held Q-x. It would also maintain a link with partner if he held a low doubleton.

It follows that when instead you lead a king, asking for a count signal, your honor holding will be stronger — headed by the A-K-J or A-K-J-10. At notrump, a king lead asks primarily that you unblock any honor that you may hold. Only when you do not hold an honor, do you give a length signal.

Let's see how this works:

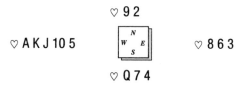

♡ 9 2

♡ A K J 10 5   ♡ 8 6 3

♡ Q 7 4

You lead the king and partner plays the three. He has not unblocked the queen, so you know that declarer holds this card. You know also that both partner and declarer hold three cards in the suit. You must switch elsewhere, seeking an entry to partner's hand for a heart lead from his side of the table. If instead partner had been dealt Q-6-3, he would have pitched the queen under your king, making it easy for you to cash the suit.

Suppose instead that partner held 8-7-4-3. He would play the seven (second best from four) and South would follow with the six. You would then at least have a chance to diagnose that South's queen was bare.

Here your strong holding is headed by the king:

♡ 7 3

♡ K Q 10 9 6 2   ♡ J 5

♡ A 8 4

Partner pitches his jack under the king and you can safely persevere with the suit. If East held A-5, he would overtake with the ace, thereby unblocking the suit, and return his remaining card through declarer's jack.

If instead East held 5-4 doubleton, he would play the five. Knowing that South held both the ace and jack, you would be alerted to the impending Bath Coup.

Signaling count when your attitude is obvious

Even when partner has led an ace or a queen, requesting an attitude signal, you should revert to a count signal when your attitude will be obvious from the cards in dummy.

◇ A K 4

◇ Q J 10 3 ◇ 8 6 2

◇ 9 7 5

Partner leads the ◇ Q against a suit contract, and dummy's ace wins the trick. You should signal count with the two. This will tell partner that you can establish a trick in the suit. With a holding such as 9-8-6-2 you would play the eight, suggesting that declarer held only a doubleton and would be able to ruff the third round.

Key points

1. Combining count and attitude signals allows you to benefit from the advantages of both. Our recommended method is to use ace and queen leads to ask for an attitude signal and king leads to request count.

2. When leading from a high honor combination (ace-king or king-queen), select the card that asks your partner for the information you are most likely to need.

3. When leading from a long suit, discovering partner's count is usually more useful than finding out about honors. You should, therefore, lead the king from long suits headed by ace-king or king-queen to ask for count.

4. When leading from short suits, particularly against notrump contracts, you need to know whether partner likes the suit. Lead the ace (from ace-king) or the queen (from king-queen) to ask for attitude.

5. In cash-out situations against high-level contracts (five level or higher), you will often lead an unsupported ace. Partner should therefore encourage only when he has the king. When you lead from ace-king against a high-level contact, lead the king for a count signal. You will then find out whether both honors will stand up.

In these problems, assume you are using our recommended 'ace for attitude, king for count' scheme of opening leads.

A.   **Dummy**
                 ♣ 10 5 4

♣ A led
            You
            ♣ Q 9 3

(N / W E / S diagram)

Partner leads the ace of clubs against a contract of four hearts. Which card will you play? Suppose the contract were five diamonds. Would this make any difference to the card you played?

B.   **You**
            ♠ A K 9 6
            ♡ J 7 2
            ◇ A K 8 3 2
            ♣ 5

You are on lead against a contract of five clubs. What will you lead and how do you plan to defend?

C.

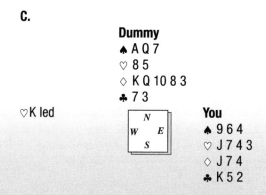

              Dummy
              ♠ A Q 7
              ♡ 8 5
              ◇ K Q 10 8 3
              ♣ 7 3

♡K led   (N / W E / S diagram)   **You**
                                          ♠ 9 6 4
                                          ♡ J 7 4 3
                                          ◇ J 7 4
                                          ♣ K 5 2

After a bidding of 1NT (15-17) -3NT, partner leads the ♡K against South's notrump game. What signal will you make?

Answers

A. When the contract is four hearts you should base your attitude signal on the assumption that partner's ace lead is from the A-K. You should therefore signal encouragement with the nine.

   If the contract were five diamonds, partner would lead the king from an A-K combination. Declarer would therefore hold the ♣K and a club continuation would be unproductive. You would play the three to discourage a further play in clubs.

B. Your general plan should be to lead the two kings in turn, requesting a count signal in each of the suits. If there is a second trick to be cashed in one of the suits, partner's signal will tell you. It is slightly better to lead the king of the shorter suit, spades, first. That's because it's more likely that either declarer or dummy will be void in the longer suit. You might have three spade tricks to take.

C. When defending a notrump contract, the lead of a king asks for the unblock of an honor, otherwise a count signal. Here you can expect partner's lead to be from ♡K-Q-10-9-x. You should unblock the jack, to let him know that he can safely continue the suit. If instead you simply give count with the seven, partner will place the declarer with the ace and jack. He will switch elsewhere.

CHAPTER 4

Suit-Preference Signals

Most of you will be familiar with the concept of the 'suit-preference' signal. You probably use it when giving partner a ruff. The idea is that leading a high card for the ruff tells partner that you have an entry in the higher of the other two suits (excluding trumps and the suit being ruffed). A low card shows a re-entry in the lower of the remaining suits. Here is a typical example:

Dummy
♠ A Q 6 4
♡ K 2
◇ K Q 7 3
♣ K Q 4

You
♠ 7 5 3
♡ J 10 7 6 3
◇ 8
♣ J 7 5 2

You lead your singleton diamond against Four Spades. To your delight, your partner wins with the ace and gives you a ruff. What do you do next?

As is the case in many good puzzles, the correct answer is, in fact, a question — which diamond did partner return at Trick 2?

If he played back the two of diamonds, you should try a club next, hoping that he holds the ace and can give you a second diamond ruff. If instead he returned the ten of diamonds at Trick 2, lead a heart next. Again, you hope to find him with the ace so that you can score the setting trick with another ruff.

The concept of the suit-preference signal is very easy and yet many pairs make use of this tool only when giving ruffs. In this chapter, we will illustrate some other scenarios in which you can use suit-preference signals. There are many of them, and this is far from being a complete treatise on the subject. We hope it will provide food for thought.

Suit-preference signals when following suit

When declarer leads a suit in which you hold only small cards, your first task is to tell partner your count. Thereafter, the order in which you play your low cards can be used for another purpose. Consider West's role in the defense on this deal:

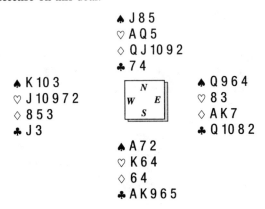

```
                    ♠ J 8 5
                    ♡ A Q 5
                    ◇ Q J 10 9 2
                    ♣ 7 4
  ♠ K 10 3          ┌─────────┐          ♠ Q 9 6 4
  ♡ J 10 9 7 2      │  N      │          ♡ 8 3
  ◇ 8 5 3           │ W    E  │          ◇ A K 7
  ♣ J 3             │    S    │          ♣ Q 10 8 2
                    └─────────┘
                    ♠ A 7 2
                    ♡ K 6 4
                    ◇ 6 4
                    ♣ A K 9 6 5
```

South opens a strong notrump and is raised to game. West leads the jack of hearts. Declarer takes this in hand with the king and plays a diamond. West signals an odd number of diamonds with the three and East allows dummy to win the trick. He is forced the take the second round of diamonds and must now decide how to continue.

There is clearly no future in a heart continuation but which black suit should he open? If West has ♠K-10-x, a spade switch will scupper the contract. If instead he holds ♣K-J-x, a club switch is required. How can East know what to do?

Yet again, the correct answer is a question: 'Which diamond did West play on the second round?'

As West showed an odd number of diamonds on the first round of the suit, he is known to have a choice at his second turn. If he followed with his lower diamond, East should switch to a club. If he played the higher one, he is showing some help in spades. This is a classic suit-preference situation. East knows from the bidding that West holds one of the black kings. The only question is which one. A suit-preference signal conveys that information.

Similar situations appear in numerous guises. Take over from East on this deal:

```
Both Vul.            ♠ K 7 4
Dealer South         ♡ J 10 4
                     ◇ 8 6 3
                     ♣ Q J 8 5
♠ A 10 3                              ♠ Q 9 8 6 2
♡ 9 7           ┌──────────┐         ♡ 8 6 3
◇ J 9 7 4 2     │    N     │         ◇ A K
♣ 9 7 3         │ W     E  │         ♣ 10 6 2
                │    S     │
                └──────────┘
                     ♠ J 5
                     ♡ A K Q 5 2
                     ◇ Q 10 5
                     ♣ A K 4
```

WEST	NORTH	EAST	SOUTH
			1♡
pass	2♡	pass	4♡
all pass			

West, your partner, leads the four of diamonds against South's heart game. After taking your two winners in the suit, you will have to reach partner's hand, so that he can cash the ◇Q or give you a diamond ruff. You win with the ace of diamonds and cash the king, playing high-low to let your partner know that you have no more diamonds. You must now hope that partner has an entry in one of the black suits. Will you try your luck with a spade or a club?

As you have probably guessed, the answer is, once again, 'Which diamond did partner play on the second round?'

Many Wests would woodenly follow with the two on the second round. 'I was letting partner know that I had five diamonds,' they would explain. Very helpful! What you need to know is where to find partner's entry. When he holds the ace of clubs, he should follow with his lowest diamond at Trick 2. With the spade ace, as in the diagram, he should play a high diamond, the jack.

Turn all the way back to the hand on Page 12. You may recall that we promised you would be able to beat the contract against all three possible layouts? This is how it can be done. When East's first card indicates that only two hearts will cash, his second card will tell you the right switch to make.

Suit-preference signals at Trick 1

Having discovered the joys of combining count and attitude signals at Trick 1, are you now ready to add suit-preference to the mix? Actually, it is not a difficult addition. It applies only when there is no conceivable future in continuing the suit that has been led. Consider this suit:

♣ A K Q

♣ J 10 9 3   N W E S   ♣ 8 5 2

♣ 7 6 4

Your partner leads the jack of clubs against a heart contract. Suppose, first, that you are playing attitude signals. Do you think your partner needs to see your signal to know that you don't have any help in clubs? Similarly, if you are playing count signals, your length in clubs is of absolutely no consequence. Choose a club spot card to pass a suit-preference signal.

What about this suit:

♢ 4

♢ A K Q 8 2   N W E S   ♢ 10 7 6 3

♢ J 9 5

Your partner leads a high diamond against a spade contract. Again, both your count and your attitude towards the suit led are irrelevant — dummy can ruff any future diamond leads. What may be vital is that your partner knows where your strength lies so that he can make the best switch at Trick 2.

The general rule to follow is to make your normal signal (count or attitude) if your side may have another trick in the suit led. In both of the examples above, the defense could take no more tricks in the led suit. Thus suit-preference took precedence over count and attitude.

Let's look at a full hand to illustrate why this can be a useful tool:

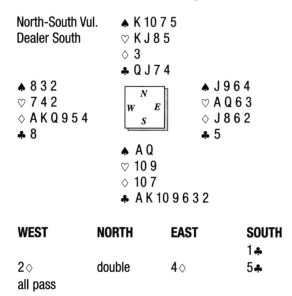

North-South Vul.
Dealer South

♠ K 10 7 5
♡ K J 8 5
♦ 3
♣ Q J 7 4

♠ 8 3 2
♡ 7 4 2
♦ A K Q 9 5 4
♣ 8

N
W E
S

♠ J 9 6 4
♡ A Q 6 3
♦ J 8 6 2
♣ 5

♠ A Q
♡ 10 9
♦ 10 7
♣ A K 10 9 6 3 2

WEST	NORTH	EAST	SOUTH
			1♣
2♦	double	4♦	5♣
all pass			

West leads the ♦K and dummy appears with a singleton in the suit. If East's method in this situation is to give count or attitude, his choice of card will not help in the slightest. West will have to guess which major suit to play next. Playing the method we advocate, suit-preference would be in operation. East would play the ♦2, a low card to suggest a heart switch rather than a spade. West would then have no guess to make and the game would go one down.

There is one other situation in which you can give a suit-preference signal at Trick 1. Take the West seat and cover the East and South cards on this deal:

Both Vul.
Dealer East

```
                    ♠ K J 8 5
                    ♡ Q 5
                    ◇ Q 10 2
                    ♣ K J 8 4
  ♠ 10 9 7 6 3      ┌─────────┐      ♠ A 4
  ♡ K               │   N     │      ♡ A J 10 8 6 4 2
  ◇ 9 7 3           │ W   E   │      ◇ 8
  ♣ 10 7 6 3        │   S     │      ♣ 9 5 2
                    └─────────┘
                    ♠ Q 2
                    ♡ 9 7 3
                    ◇ A K J 6 5 4
                    ♣ A Q
```

WEST	NORTH	EAST	SOUTH
		3♡	4◇
pass	5◇	all pass	

You lead the king of hearts, winning the first trick (East cannot afford to overtake in case you have a doubleton). What do you do at Trick 2? Will it help if your partner has played an encouraging heart on your ace? What if he has played a count card showing an odd number of hearts? Neither will help in the slightest. You need to know how to reach partner's hand and the only way to get this type of decision right consistently is for partner to give you a suit-preference signal at Trick 1. He should play a high heart if he has the ace of spades, as in the diagram, and a low heart if his entry is in clubs.

Why is this a suit-preference situation? East knows that if you hold a second heart you will lead it at Trick 2, regardless of the signal he gives. A singleton king is a possibility, though, and in that case you may need some help to determine the best switch.

Key points

1. In suit-preference situations, playing a low card shows interest in the lower of the remaining suits, a high card interest in the higher.

2. When you have already given a count signal on the first round of a suit, your second card may be used to pass a suit-preference message.

3. A spot card at Trick 1 carries a suit-preference message only when there is no possible second trick for the defenders in the suit led. For example, West leads a side-suit ace and dummy goes down with king doubleton.

QUIZ

A. ♡ K 5 3

♡ A led  ♡ Q 9 6 2

♡ unknown

i) Partner leads the ♡A against a 4♠ contract requesting an attitude signal. Do you signal suit preference or attitude?

ii) If partner continues with a second heart, won with the king, what do you then signal?

B. ♣ K 7

♣ A led 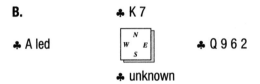 ♣ Q 9 6 2

♣ unknown

Partner leads the ♣A against a 4♡ contract requesting an attitude signal. Do you signal suit preference or attitude?

C. ♠ A K 3

♠ J 10 8 5 2

You lead the ♠J against a heart contract. Declarer wins with dummy's king. He then cashes the ace of spades, discarding a club from his hand. How should you follow to this trick?

D. ◇ A K Q 6

◇ 9 led  ◇ 10 7 4 2

◇ unknown

Partner leads the nine of diamonds against a spade contract. How should you signal?

Answers

A. i) You should signal encouragement with the nine. Since your side has the possibility of a second trick in the suit, there is no reason for your card to be read as suit preference.

ii) Give a suit-preference signal. If partner began with ♡A-x, which is likely, he will need to know how to put you on lead to cash your ♡Q.

B. Give a suit-preference signal at Trick 1. Your side can score no more club tricks, so attitude in clubs takes a back seat to more important matters — which of the other side suits should partner attack at Trick 2?

C. Partner knows your exact spade holding, so count and attitude are irrelevant. Give a suit preference signal — a high spade to show interest in diamonds and a low one to show a preference for clubs.

D. Give a suit-preference signal. It is clear that your side has no future in diamonds. Help partner to find a more profitable line of attack next time he gains the lead.

Discarding

In all the examples we have seen so far, you have been signaling while following suit. When discarding, your scope for providing partner with useful information is wider — you can choose not only a high card or a low card, but also which suit to throw.

The limitations of attitude discards

Most players are taught simple 'attitude discards' as novices. In this method a high discard encourages the lead of that suit, a low discard discourages it. Indeed, many people continue using this system even when they become more experienced. There are two primary problems with it.

The first is that you may have to throw a card you can ill afford, in order to persuade partner to lead your suit. Suppose you are defending a notrump contract and you want partner to switch to your handsome ♠KQ1084. If you throw an encouraging ten or eight of spades, and a spade switch subsequently sets up the suit, you will have wasted one of your winners.

The second problem is that partner may be unable to tell whether your card is high or low.

The limitations of suit-preference discards

There are various discarding methods based on suit-preference principles — McKenney or Lavinthal (the name depends on which side of the Atlantic you are from) is the most common.

These methods work in a similar way to the suit-preference signals discussed in the previous chapter. Suppose you are defending a notrump contract and declarer is cashing diamond winners. A discard of one of the other three suits means 'I don't like this suit'. The size of your discard tells partner which of the other suits you do like. For example, if you threw a high spade, this would mean that you liked hearts; a low spade would indicate interest in clubs. If instead you threw a club, a high card would ask for spades, a low one for hearts.

The main problem encountered by users of this method is that every discard appears to pass a positive message: 'I would like a switch to such-and-such a suit.' What are you meant to do if you have the kings of two different suits? What if you have the queen of one suit, but don't actually want partner to switch to that suit because it will assist declarer to find the queen? Many are the cries of, 'But you asked for a heart!'

Let's take a look at a full hand to see why playing suit-preference discards may present a problem:

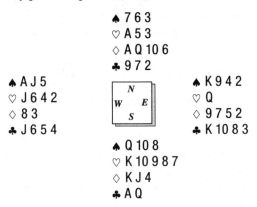

♠ 7 6 3
♡ A 5 3
♢ A Q 10 6
♣ 9 7 2

♠ A J 5
♡ J 6 4 2
♢ 8 3
♣ J 6 5 4

♠ K 9 4 2
♡ Q
♢ 9 7 5 2
♣ K 10 8 3

♠ Q 10 8
♡ K 10 9 8 7
♢ K J 4
♣ A Q

West leads a passive diamond against South's 4♡. Declarer wins and plays ace, king and another trump to West's jack. What suit preference discard should East give?

If he held ♠K-Q-x-x and nothing in clubs, all would be easy. He would throw the ♢9 or the ♣8 and a spade switch would defeat the contract. Holding the kings of both black suits, he is somewhat stuck.

The major problem with playing McKenney-type discards is that you have to make the decision. You must signal for one suit or the other. Think back (way back) to our earlier discussion of attitude signals. One of the major drawbacks was that you had to make a decision — encourage or discourage — even when you did not have sufficient information to make that choice. The same applies to suit-preference discards.

The message that you really want to send on this hand is: 'I have something in both black suits — switch to the one in which you also have honors.' Playing suit-preference discards, this is not an option.

Throw Losers, Keep Winners

You may be surprised to hear that we recommend a very simple method of discarding — simply throwing from a suit you do not want. Surely such a simple method cannot possibly be better than all the clever alternatives... Or can it?

Let's see how it works on the deal in the previous section. Since you cannot tell which black suit to request, you would simply discard two diamonds, denying interest in that suit but expressing no preference between the black suits. Partner can then work out that you have a similar holding in both clubs and spades. If you have no black honor or the two queens, the contract cannot be beaten. He will therefore be forced to assume you hold both kings. Armed with that knowledge, it will not be difficult for partner to find the required switch to a low spade.

If instead you held strong spades and clearly wanted a spade switch, your first discard would be a club. With the luxury of a second discard, you would next throw a diamond.

If you wanted a club switch, you would throw a spade then a diamond. You could even suggest a diamond continuation, by throwing once from each black suit.

Note that the size of the card you throw is irrelevant in terms of its primary message, i.e. where your strength lies. That information is transmitted by which suit or suit(s) that you discard. You can therefore select your spot card from the chosen suit to give count. A discard such as the ♣8 would mean that you did not like clubs and you had an even number of cards in the suit. Quite a bit of information to be passing with just a single card!

Key points

1. Be wary of discarding methods where it is the size of the card thrown that transmits the primary message. You will not always have the right spot card to convey your message. Alternative methods such as 'Reverse attitude' or 'Odd/Even' do not solve this problem — they merely fail to work on different combinations of spot cards.

2. Be wary of methods in which you *must* signal for one suit or another. You will not always be able to tell which suit you want partner to play.

3. We recommend the method 'throw from a suit you do not want, giving count at the same time'. Good methods need not be complicated.

CHAPTER 6

Other Types of Signal

Signals in the trump suit

What does it mean if you play high-low in the trump suit? For many decades, and still today, this is the message:

A **trump echo** shows three trumps and an ability to ruff.

Let's see a typical example of its use:

```
              ♠ Q 7 4
              ♡ A 9 3
              ◇ A K Q J 9
              ♣ Q 2
 ♠ 8 5 2                      ♠ K J
 ♡ 10 6 4 2      N            ♡ J 8 5
 ◇ 7         W       E        ◇ 10 8 6 5 3
 ♣ K 8 6 5 4     S            ♣ J 10 3
              ♠ A 10 9 6 3
              ♡ K Q 7
              ◇ 4 2
              ♣ A 9 7
```

Your partner leads the ◇7 against South's small slam in spades. Declarer wins in dummy and plays a trump to your jack and his ace. You win the second round of trumps with the king and must decide what to do next.

If partner has both a singleton diamond and a third trump, you can defeat the contract by giving him a ruff. If declarer has the singleton diamond or partner started with only two trumps, returning a diamond could be fatal. Perhaps partner holds the ♣A or declarer does not have enough discards on the diamonds unless you give him an extra trick by returning that suit now.

This problem is solved by agreeing to play the 'trump echo'. On the actual layout, West will play high-low on the first two rounds of trumps, thereby showing both the ability to ruff diamonds and a third trump. If instead West played upwards in trumps, East would know that he should look elsewhere for the second defensive trick.

Here is a slightly more sophisticated use of the trump echo:

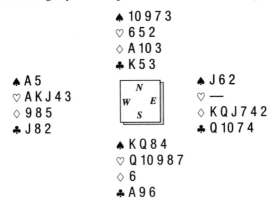

Defending three spades, you start with two top hearts and a heart ruff. Declarer wins partner's ◇K return in the dummy and plays a trump to the king and your ace. How do you score the setting trick?

If declarer has a second diamond, you can simply play that suit to partner's queen. If declarer began with only one diamond, you will need a second heart ruff. Can partner overruff dummy's ten of spades?

Again, East should provide you with the answer by signaling in trumps. With his actual holding, he should ruff the third round of hearts with the six, then complete his high-low when declarer plays a trump to your ace. This trump echo tells you that partner can overruff dummy.

If East's did not hold the jack of trumps he would play upwards in trumps, despite holding three trumps. You would then have to hope that declarer held a second diamond.

The Smith Echo

We conclude with a brief look at a useful signaling tool employed by many tournament partnerships — the Smith Echo. It is used primarily against notrump contracts. The idea is that when you follow to the first suit played by declarer you convey information not about that suit but about the suit led at Trick 1.

There are different ways to play the convention, but the version we describe here is the original and as good as any of the alternatives. We start by looking at the Smith Echo given by the partner of the opening leader. For example, perhaps this suit is led:

```
                ◇ A 6 5
                 ┌─────┐
                 │  N  │
 ◇ 10 8 7 4 2    │W   E│      ◇ Q J 3
                 │  S  │
                 └─────┘
                ◇ K 9
```

West leads the ◇4 and your jack is won by declarer's king. At this stage West has no idea who holds the queen — South might have started with K-Q-9 in the suit. When declarer plays on one of his own suits next, a high-low by East will be a Smith Echo, designed to enlighten West as to the position in the suit originally led.

A Smith Echo by the non-leader means: 'I have an unexpectedly good holding in your suit. Please continue it.'

So, East would echo in declarer's first suit when he held the queen of hearts, play his cards upwards without it. Playing Smith Echoes means that you cannot signal your count in the suit led. Only in the 'long suit in an entryless dummy' situation will you revert to giving partner a count on that suit.

The Smith Echo is a useful tool but it really comes into its own when used from the opening leader's seat. Consider East's problem on this deal:

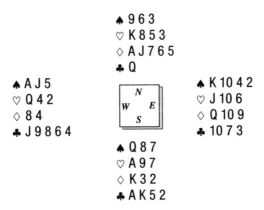

```
              ♠ 9 6 3
              ♡ K 8 5 3
              ◇ A J 7 6 5
              ♣ Q
♠ A J 5                          ♠ K 10 4 2
♡ Q 4 2        ┌─────┐          ♡ J 10 6
◇ 8 4         │  N  │          ◇ Q 10 9
♣ J 9 8 6 4   │ W  E │          ♣ 10 7 3
              │  S  │
              └─────┘
              ♠ Q 8 7
              ♡ A 9 7
              ◇ K 3 2
              ♣ A K 5 2
```

Your partner leads the ♣6 against 3NT. Declarer wins with dummy's queen, crosses to his king of diamonds, and finesses the diamond jack to your queen. What do you do now?

On the actual layout, a spade switch nets four more tricks for the defense — one down. But could not the full hand just as easily be something like:

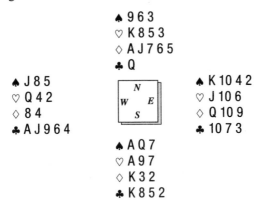

```
              ♠ 9 6 3
              ♡ K 8 5 3
              ◇ A J 7 6 5
              ♣ Q
♠ J 8 5                          ♠ K 10 4 2
♡ Q 4 2        ┌─────┐          ♡ J 10 6
◇ 8 4         │  N  │          ◇ Q 10 9
♣ A J 9 6 4   │ W  E │          ♣ 10 7 3
              │  S  │
              └─────┘
              ♠ A Q 7
              ♡ A 9 7
              ◇ K 3 2
              ♣ K 8 5 2
```

Now, if you return a spade when you win the queen of diamonds, declarer will take the finesse and claim nine tricks. Partner will not exactly be overjoyed at your imaginative switch.

Smith Echoes can help to solve these situations too.

A Smith Echo by the opening leader means: 'I have an unexpectedly poor holding in the suit I led. Consider a switch.'

West would echo in diamonds on the first hand but play them upwards on the second. Problem solved!

....

More Bridge Titles from Master Point Press

Bridge, Zia... and me by Michael Rosenberg (foreword by Zia Mahmood)
192pp., PB   Can $19.95   US $15.95

Classic Kantar *A collection of bridge humor* by Eddie Kantar
192pp., PB   Can $19.95   US $14.95

Competitive Bidding in the 21st Century by Marshall Miles
254pp.,PB   Can. $22.95   US. $16.95

Countdown to Winning Bridge by Tim Bourke and Marc Smith
92pp., PB   Can $19.95   US $14.95

Easier Done Than Said *Brilliancy at the Bridge Table*
by Prakash K. Paranjape
128pp., PB   Can $15.95   US $12.95

For Love or Money *The Life of a Bridge Journalist*
by Mark Horton and Brian Senior (Foreword by Omar Sharif)
189pp., PB   Can $22.95   US $16.95

I Shot my Bridge Partner by Matthew Granovetter
384pp., PB   Can $19.95   US $14.95

Murder at the Bridge Table by Matthew Granovetter
320pp., PB   Can $19.95   US $14.95

Partnership Bidding *A Workbook* by Mary Paul
96pp., PB   Can $9.95   US $7.95

Playing With The Bridge Legends by Barnet Shenkin
(forewords by Zia and Michael Rosenberg)
192pp., PB   Can $22.95   US $16.95

Saints and Sinners: *The St. Titus Bridge Challenge*
by David Bird & Tim Bourke
192pp., PB   Can $19.95   US $14.95

Tales out of School *'Bridge 101' and other stories* by David Silver
(foreword by Dorothy Hayden Truscott)
128pp., PB   Can $ 12.95   US $9.95

The Bridge Player's Bedside Book edited by Tony Forrester
256pp., HC   Can $27.95   US $19.95

The Complete Book of BOLS Bridge Tips edited by Sally Brock
176pp., PB (photographs)   Can $24.95   US$17.95

There Must Be A Way... *52 challenging bridge hands*
by Andrew Diosy (foreword by Eddie Kantar)
96pp., PB $9.95 US & Can.

You Have to See This... *52 more challenging bridge problems*
by Andrew Diosy and Linda Lee
96pp., PB   Can $12.95   US $9.95

World Class — *Conversations with the Bridge Masters* by Marc Smith
288pp., PB (photographs)   Can $24.95   US $17.95